quick time
dishes

quick time

Published by:
TRIDENT PRESS INTERNATIONAL
801 12th Avenue South, Suite 400
Naples, Fl 34102 USA
Tel: + 1 239 649 7077
Email: tridentpress@worldnet.att.net
Websites: www.trident-international.com
www.chefexpressinternational.com

Quik Time Dishes
© Trident Press International

Publisher
Simon St. John Bailey

Editor-in-chief
Isabel Toyos

Includes Index
ISBN 1582797692
UPC 6 15269 97692 0

2004 Edition
Printed in Colombia by Cargraphics S.A.

introduction

The recipes in this book have been planned
to help you prepare and serve a delicious
family meal in less than an hour. Use these
hints and tips to save time.

- As you are planning meals check your pantry shelves, refrigerator and freezer. Remember if you are running low on your staples replace them before you run out.

- Writing a shopping list saves time and money. Make a master list and do your shopping once a week so you don't have the bother of last-minute shopping trips and you can avoid the rush hour.

- Get to know the layout of the supermarket and write shopping list according to it. Grouping ingredients in their categories, such as meats, dairy products, canned foods and frozen foods saves backtracking.

- When possible, purchase food in the form it is used in the recipe. Ask your butcher to cut, slice or bone out cuts of meat according to the preparation requirements.

- Look for new and interesting convenience products such as sauces and dressings, prepared pastries and pastry cases, canned fruits and vegetables and dessert items.

- Buy grated cheese, bottled minced garlic, minced ginger and minced chilies. These save having to crush, chop and grate when time is short.

- Store frozen meals in containers that can go straight from the freezer into the microwave, to the table and then into the dishwasher.

- Transfer frozen meat and poultry to the refrigerator the night before so that it thaws for dinner the next night.

- Collect all ingredients before starting to cook –this saves time and ensures you have everything you need.

- A food processor is the ultimate time saver in the kitchen. Ingredients can be grated, shredded, chopped, blended, mixed and puréed in a fraction of the time it takes to do it by hand.

- Use prepared whipped cream for quick dessert decoration ideas. Long-life cream is also a handy pantry item.

- Keep a selection of bread in the freezer. It defrosts quickly and is a good accompaniment to a meal.

Difficulty scale

■□□ I Easy to do

■■□ I Requires attention

■■■ I Requires experience

the blta
(bacon, lettuce, tomato and avocado)

■□□ | Cooking time: 5 minutes - Preparation time: 10 minutes

ingredients
> 12 rashers bacon, rind removed
> 8 slices white bread, toasted
> 4 tablespoons mayonnaise
> 4 iceberg or cos lettuce leaves
> 1 ripe avocado, halved, stoned and sliced
> 2 large tomatoes, cut into 12 slices
> freshly ground black pepper

method
1. Grill or fry bacon for 4-5 minutes or until crisp. Drain on absorbent kitchen paper and set aside.
2. Spread each slice of toast with mayonnaise.
3. Divide lettuce, bacon, avocado and tomatoes evenly between four slices of toast. Season to taste with black pepper and top with remaining toast slices. Serve immediately.

....
Serves 4

tip from the chef
Try making this variation of the popular BLT (bacon, lettuce and tomato sandwich) with pastrami or ham as interesting and easy alternatives to the bacon.

new york
reuben

■□□ I Cooking time: 10 minutes - Preparation time: 10 minutes

method

1. Place sauerkraut between sheets of absorbent kitchen paper and squeeze to remove as much moisture as possible.
2. Place bread slices under a preheated hot grill and toast on one side.
3. Spread untoasted side of each bread slice with dressing, then top with a generous layer of sauerkraut, 2 slices corned beef and a slice Swiss cheese.
4. Return to grill and cook for 3-4 minutes longer or until topping is heated through and cheese melts. Serve immediately.

ingredients

> **220 g/7 oz canned or bottled sauerkraut, drained and rinsed in cold water**
> **4 thick slices rye bread**
> **4 tablespoons Thousand Island dressing**
> **8 slices corned beef**
> **4 slices Swiss cheese**

Serves 4

tip from the chef

First created by Reuben's Restaurant in New York there are now as many versions of this famous New York sandwich as there are chefs who make it.

sun & moon

ingredients

sunny chicken rolls

> 1/2 cup/125 ml/4 fl oz mayonnaise
> 2 tablespoons vinaigrette dressing
> 1 teaspoon French mustard
> 1 cooked chicken, skinned, boned and cut into small pieces
> 2 eating apples, peeled, cored and diced
> 2 hard-boiled eggs, diced
> 2 stalks celery, sliced thinly
> 2 spring onions, shredded
> 1 tablespoon chopped fresh parsley
> freshly ground black pepper
> 4 large crusty bread rolls, split

salmon moons

> 155 g/5 oz cream cheese, softened
> 1/4 cup/60 g/2 oz sour cream
> 155 g/5 oz sliced smoked salmon, chopped
> 1 spring onion, thinly sliced
> 3 teaspoons chopped fresh dill
> 2 teaspoons capers, drained and chopped
> 2 teaspoons lime or lemon juice
> 4 croissants, split

method

1. To make rolls, place mayonnaise, dressing and mustard in a bowl and mix to combine. Add chicken, apples, eggs, celery, spring onions and parsley. Season to taste with black pepper and toss to combine. Top bases of rolls with mixture, then place other halves on top.

2. To make croissants, place cream cheese and sour cream into a bowl and beat until smooth. Add salmon, spring onion, dill, capers and lime or lemon juice and mix to combine. Top bottom half of each croissant with mixture, then place other halves on top.

....

Serves 4

tip from the chef

For a tropical chicken filling, add 125 g/4 oz canned diced mangoes or peaches.
Canned red or pink salmon, drained and mashed, is a more economical alternative to the smoked salmon.

curried
pasta salad

■□□ | Cooking time: 10 minutes - Preparation time: 15 minutes

method

1. Cook pasta in boiling water in a large saucepan following packet directions. Drain, rinse under cold running water and cool completely.
2. Boil, steam or microwave broccoli and carrots separately until just tender. Drain and refresh under cold running water. Drain again and place in a serving bowl. Add zucchini, red pepper, spring onions and pasta and toss to combine.
3. To make dressing, place mayonnaise, mustard, lemon juice, curry powder and black pepper to taste in a bowl and mix to combine. Spoon dressing over salad and toss to combine. Serve at room temperature.

....

Serves 4

ingredients

> 250 g/8 oz macaroni
> 250 g/8 oz broccoli, cut into small florets
> 2 carrots, cut into matchsticks
> 2 zucchini, cut into matchsticks
> 1 red pepper, cut into thin strips
> 2 spring onions, thinly sliced

curry dressing

> 4 tablespoons mayonnaise
> 1 tablespoon French mustard
> 1 tablespoon lemon juice
> 1/2 teaspoon curry powder
> freshly ground black pepper

tip from the chef

This dish makes a great vegetarian main meal when served with a tossed green salad and crusty bread or serve it as an accompaniment to grilled chicken or meat.

pesto pasta

■□□ | Cooking time: 10 minutes - Preparation time: 10 minutes

ingredients

> **500 g/1 lb fettuccine or other pasta of your choice**

basil and garlic pesto
> **1 large bunch fresh basil**
> **1/2 bunch fresh parsley**
> **60 g/2 oz grated Parmesan or Romano cheese**
> **30 g/1 oz pine nuts or almonds**
> **2 large cloves garlic, quartered**
> **freshly ground black pepper**
> **1/3 cup/90 ml/3 fl oz olive oil**

method

1. To make pesto, place basil leaves, parsley, Parmesan or Romano cheese, pine nuts or almonds, garlic and black pepper to taste in a food processor or blender and process to finely chop. With machine running, slowly add oil and continue processing to make a smooth paste.

2. Cook pasta in boiling water in a large saucepan following packet directions. Drain and divide between serving bowls, top with pesto, toss to combine and serve immediately.

....
Serves 4

tip from the chef

Spinach pesto makes a tasty alternative when fresh basil is unavailable. To make, use fresh spinach in place of the basil and add 1 teaspoon dried basil.

pasta putanesca

■☐☐ I Cooking time: 20 minutes - Preparation time: 10 minutes

method

1. Cook pasta in boiling water in a large saucepan following packet directions. Drain, set aside and keep warm.
2. To make sauce, heat oil in a saucepan over a low heat, add garlic and cook, stirring, for 2 minutes. Add tomatoes and bring to the boil, then stir in anchovies, black olives, capers, oregano and chili powder and simmer for 3 minutes longer. Spoon sauce over hot pasta, sprinkle with parsley and Parmesan cheese and serve.

....
Serves 6

ingredients

> 500 g/1 lb linguine or thin spaghetti

putanesca sauce

> 2 tablespoons olive oil
> 5 cloves garlic, crushed
> 4 x 440 g/14 oz canned peeled Italian plum tomatoes, drained and chopped
> 6 anchovy fillets, coarsely chopped
> 60 g/2 oz stoned black olives
> 2 tablespoons capers, drained and chopped
> 1 teaspoon dried oregano
> $1/4$ teaspoon chili powder
> $1/2$ bunch parsley, coarsely chopped
> 30 g/1 oz grated Parmesan cheese

tip from the chef

The reserved juice from the tomatoes can be frozen and used in a casserole or soup at a later date.

noodles
with coconut sauce

■■□ | Cooking time: 20 minutes - Preparation time: 15 minutes

method

1. Cook noodles in boiling water in a large saucepan following packet directions. Drain, rinse under hot water and place in a large serving bowl.

2. To make sauce, heat oil in a saucepan over a medium heat, add onions and cook, stirring, for 5 minutes or until onions are tender. Add garlic, coriander root, if using, chilies, curry powder, cinnamon and cardamom and cook, stirring, for 1 minute or until fragrant.

3. Stir in coconut milk, bring to simmering and simmer, uncovered, for 5 minutes. Remove pan from heat, pour sauce over hot noodles and toss to combine. Sprinkle with fresh coriander and serve immediately.

....
Serves 4

ingredients

> 500 g/1 lb fresh egg noodles

coconut curry sauce
> 2 tablespoons vegetable oil
> 2 onions, diced
> 2 cloves garlic, crushed
> 2 teaspoons finely chopped fresh coriander root (optional)
> 2 small fresh red chilies, seeded and finely chopped
> 2 teaspoons curry powder
> 1/2 teaspoon ground cinnamon
> 1/4 teaspoon ground cardamom
> 1 1/2 cups/375 ml/ 12 fl oz coconut milk
> 2 tablespoons coarsely chopped fresh coriander

tip from the chef

If you grow your own coriander you will have no trouble obtaining fresh coriander root and fortunately fresh coriander is usually sold with it roots still on. The heat of this dish can be adjusted by using more or less chilies.

crusty
corn soufflé

■■□ I Cooking time: 45 minutes - Preparation time: 15 minutes

ingredients
> **60 g/2 oz butter**
> **1/4 cup/30 g/1 oz flour**
> **440 g/14 oz canned creamed sweet corn**
> **4 eggs, separated**
> **3 spring onions, chopped**
> **2 tablespoons finely chopped parsley**
> **freshly ground black pepper**
> **60 g/2 oz grated tasty cheese (mature Cheddar)**

method
1. Melt butter in a saucepan over a medium heat, add flour and cook, stirring, for 1 minute. Stir in sweet corn and cook for 1 minute longer. Remove pan from heat and set aside to cool for 5 minutes.
2. Beat egg yolks, one at a time, into sauce mixture. Stir in spring onions, parsley and black pepper to taste.
3. Place egg whites in a clean bowl and beat until stiff peaks form. Fold egg whites into corn mixture.
4. Spoon mixture into an ungreased 2 litre/ 3½ pt soufflé dish, sprinkle with cheese and bake at 200°C/400°F/Gas 6 for 10 minutes. Reduce oven temperature to 180°C/350°F/Gas 4 and bake for 30 minutes or until soufflé is well risen and golden.

....

Serves 4

tip from the chef
This soufflé is delicious served with salsa fresca (page 27) and a tossed green salad.

ratatouille

■□□ | Cooking time: 40 minutes - Preparation time: 15 minutes

method

1. Heat oil in a large saucepan over a medium heat, add onions and cook, stirring, for 5 minutes or until onions are lightly browned. Add green peppers and garlic and cook, stirring occasionally, for 5 minutes longer.
2. Add zucchini, eggplant, tomatoes, oregano, basil and marjoram and bring to the boil. Reduce heat and simmer, stirring occasionally, for 30 minutes or until mixture reduces and thickens and vegetables are well cooked. Season to taste with black pepper. Serve hot, warm or at room temperature.

....
Serves 6

ingredients

> 1/4 cup/60 ml/2 fl oz vegetable oil
> 2 onions, chopped
> 2 green peppers, diced
> 2 cloves garlic, crushed
> 4 zucchini, diced
> 2 eggplant, diced
> 2 x 440 g/14 oz canned tomatoes, undrained and mashed
> 1 teaspoon dried oregano
> 1 teaspoon dried basil
> 1 teaspoon dried marjoram
> freshly ground black pepper

tip from the chef

Red peppers, mushrooms and fresh herbs are all tasty additions to this popular dish. With the addition of canned beans this becomes a great main meal for vegetarians. Drain and rinse the beans and add to the vegetable mixture in the last 5 minutes of cooking.

spicy vegetable burgers

■□□ | Cooking time: 10 minutes - Preparation time: 20 minutes

method

1. To make burgers, place beans in a bowl and using a fork mash well. Add breadcrumbs, carrot, spring onion, parsley, ground garlic, spice mix, egg and black pepper to taste and mix well to combine.

2. Shape mixture into 6 patties. Place on a plate lined with plastic food wrap and chill for 10-15 minutes.

3. Heat 1 cm/¹/2 in oil in a frying pan over a medium heat, add patties and cook for 3-4 minutes each side or until golden and heated through.

4. To assemble, place a lettuce leaf on bottom half of each muffin, top with a pattie, a spoonful salsa and top half of muffin.

....

Makes 6

ingredients

> **6 English muffins, split and toasted**
> **6 lettuce leaves**
> **6 tablespoons bottled tomato salsa or salsa fresca (page 27)**

spicy burgers

> **440 g/14 oz canned soy beans, rinsed and drained**
> **1 cup/125 g/4 oz dried breadcrumbs**
> **1 carrot, grated**
> **1 spring onion, chopped**
> **1 tablespoon chopped fresh parsley**
> **¹/2 teaspoon dried ground garlic**
> **¹/2 teaspoon Cajun spice mix**
> **1 egg, beaten**
> **freshly ground black pepper**
> **vegetable oil**

tip from the chef

Keeping a selection of bread, rolls and muffins in the freezer ensures that you always have a quick basis to an easy meal such as this one. Also remember that bread makes a quick and nutritious accompaniment to a meal.

potato latkes
with salsa fresca

■ □ □ | Cooking time: 10 minutes - Preparation time: 15 minutes

method

1. Place potatoes, onion, flour, eggs and black pepper to taste in a food processor (a) and process to finely chop potatoes and combine ingredients.
2. Heat 1 cm/^{1}/$_2$ in oil in a large frying pan over a medium heat. Cook tablespoons of potato mixture in oil for 3-4 minutes each side (b) or until golden. Drain on absorbent kitchen paper and serve immediately.
3. To make salsa, place tomatoes, coriander, chilies, lemon juice and black pepper to taste in a bowl and toss to combine (c). Stand at room temperature for at least 15 minutes before serving.

....

Serves 6

tip from the chef

Finely chopped herbs such as parsley, dill, coriander or thyme can be added to latkes mixture to create different flavors.
Salsa fresca is a tasty accompaniment to simply cooked meat and chicken dishes, as well as dishes such as ranch-style eggs (page 28).

ingredients

> **3 large potatoes, peeled and roughly chopped**
> **1 onion, roughly chopped**
> **2 tablespoons flour**
> **2 eggs**
> **freshly ground black pepper**
> **vegetable oil**

salsa fresca
> **4 large ripe tomatoes, coarsely chopped**
> **3 tablespoons finely chopped fresh coriander**
> **2 fresh green chilies, seeded and finely chopped**
> **1 tablespoon lemon juice**
> **1 teaspoon freshly ground pepper**

a

b

c

ranch-style eggs

■□□ | Cooking time: 20 minutes - Preparation time: 5 minutes

ingredients

> **30 g/1 oz butter**
> **1 small onion, thinly sliced**
> **440 g/14 oz canned tomatoes, drained and mashed**
> **1 fresh green chili, seeded and cut into thin strips**
> **2 tablespoons tomato paste (purée)**
> **4 eggs**
> **freshly ground black pepper**
> **125 g/4 oz grated tasty cheese (mature Cheddar)**
> **2 tablespoons chopped fresh coriander**

method

1. Melt butter in a heavy-based frying pan over a medium heat, add onion and cook, stirring, for 3-4 minutes or until onion is soft, but not brown. Stir in tomatoes, chili and tomato paste (a), bring to simmering and simmer, stirring occasionally, for 10 minutes.

2. Using the back of a large spoon, make 4 hollows in the tomato mixture (b). Break an egg into a cup, then carefully slide into one of the hollows (c). Repeat with remaining eggs. Cover pan and cook for 5 minutes or until egg whites are just set.

3. Season eggs with black pepper and sprinkle with cheese (d). Re-cover pan and cook for 2 minutes longer or until cheese melts and eggs are cooked to your liking. Sprinkle with coriander and serve immediately.

....
Serves 4

tip from the chef

For a complete meal serve with a tossed green salad and crusty bread or rolls. For the best results use a well-seasoned cast iron frying pan when making this dish.

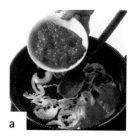

a

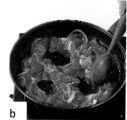

b

c

d

french
fried camembert

■□□ | Cooking time: 10 minutes - Preparation time: 5 minutes

method

1. Cut each Camembert round into 3 wedges. Dip each wedge in egg then roll in breadcrumbs to coat.
2. Heat 2.5 cm/1 in oil in a frying pan over a medium heat, until a cube of bread dropped in browns in 50 seconds. Add cheese wedges and cook for 3-4 minutes each side or until golden. Drain on absorbent kitchen paper and serve immediately with jam and crème fraîche.

ingredients

> **2 x 125 g/4 oz rounds Camembert cheese, well chilled**
> **1 egg, beaten**
> **1 cup/125 g/4 oz dried breadcrumbs**
> **vegetable oil**
> **black cherry jam**
> **crème fraîche**

....

Serves 6

tip from the chef

The triangles can be prepared ahead of time and refrigerated until just prior to cooking. It is important that the cheese is well chilled before cooking or it will melt and collapse when added to the pan.

fillets
of fish florentine

■ ■ ■ | Cooking time: 40 minutes - Preparation time: 25 minutes

ingredients
> **6 firm white fish fillets**
> **1/4 cup/60 ml/2 fl oz lemon juice**
> **1 tablespoon vegetable oil**
> **1 onion, diced**
> **250 g/8 oz frozen chopped spinach, thawed and squeezed**
> **1 tablespoon dry sherry**
> **pinch ground cinnamon**
> **100 g/3 1/2 oz cottage cheese, drained**
> **75 g/2 1/2 oz feta cheese, crumbled**
> **75 g/2 1/2 oz Brie, diced (optional)**
> **freshly ground black pepper**
> **1/2 cup/125 ml/4 fl oz chicken stock**
> **1/4 cup/30 g/1 oz dried breadcrumbs**
> **30 g/1 oz grated Parmesan cheese**

method
1. Place fish fillets in a glass or ceramic dish, pour over lemon juice and marinate for 5 minutes.
2. Heat oil in a frying pan over a medium heat, add onion and cook, stirring, for 5 minutes or until onion is soft. Add spinach and cook, stirring, for 3 minutes longer. Stir in sherry and cinnamon, remove pan from heat and set aside to cool.
3. Stir cottage cheese, feta cheese, Brie, if using, and black pepper to taste into spinach mixture and mix to combine.
4. Drain fish and place a heaped spoonful of spinach mixture at one end of each fillet then roll up loosely. Place fish rolls seam side down in an ovenproof dish and pour over stock.
5. Combine breadcrumbs and Parmesan cheese, sprinkle over fish and bake at 200°C/400°F/Gas 6 for 25-30 minutes or until fish is cooked when tested with a fork.

. . . .

Serves 6

tip from the chef

Goat's cheese is a tasty alternative to the feta cheese in this recipe.

cajun
blackened fish

■□□ | Cooking time: 10 minutes - Preparation time: 15 minutes

method

1. Brush each fish fillet liberally with melted butter.
2. Combine spice mix, paprika and chili powder and using your hands, rub spice mixture evenly over fillets.
3. Heat a large cast iron frying pan over a high heat until very hot. Add fish fillets and cook for 1-2 minutes each side or until fish flakes when tested with a fork. Serve immediately with any remaining melted butter.

....
Serves 6

ingredients

> **6 firm white fish fillets, each about 2 cm/3/4 in thick**
> **100 g/3 1/2 oz unsalted butter, melted**
> **1 1/2 tablespoons Cajun spice mix**
> **1 teaspoon paprika**
> **1/4 teaspoon chili powder**

tip from the chef

It may be necessary to cook the fish in batches for this recipe. Shelled and deveined uncooked prawns are also delicious prepared in this way.

bengal
fish with yogurt

■□□ | Cooking time: 10 minutes - Preparation time: 10 minutes

ingredients

> **4 large uncooked prawns, shelled, deveined and coarsely chopped**
> **2 spring onions, chopped**
> **1 large clove garlic, crushed**
> **1 small fresh red chili, seeded and finely chopped**
> **1/4 cup/45 g/1 1/2 oz natural yogurt**
> **2 tablespoons vegetable oil**
> **4 firm white fish fillets**

method

1. Place prawns, spring onions, garlic, chili and yogurt in a bowl and mix to combine. Set aside.
2. Brush a flameproof shallow dish with oil. Place fish in a single layer in the dish. Place under a preheated hot grill and cook for 4-5 minutes. Turn fish over, top with yogurt mixture and cook for 4-5 minutes longer or until fish is cooked when tested with a fork. Serve immediately.

....

Serves 4

tip from the chef

This is also a tasty way of preparing chicken breast fillets, but remember to allow extra cooking time.

chicken tacos

■ ■ □ | Cooking time: 15 minutes - Preparation time: 15 minutes

method

1. To make filling, heat oil in a saucepan over a medium heat, add onion and cook, stirring, for 5 minutes or until onion is soft. Add garlic and cook for 1 minute longer.
2. Add chicken and cook, stirring, for 4-5 minutes or until chicken is brown and crumbly. Stir in chili powder, water, tomato paste (purée) and black pepper to taste, cover and cook, stirring occasionally, for 5 minutes. Stir in coriander.
3. Divide filling evenly between taco shells, top with lettuce, tomatoes, onion and cheese and accompany with salsa.

....
Serves 6

ingredients

- > **12 taco shells, warmed**
- > **1/2 head lettuce, shredded**
- > **2 tomatoes, chopped**
- > **1 red onion, finely chopped**
- > **125 g/4 oz grated tasty cheese (mature Cheddar)**
- > **4 tablespoons bottled tomato salsa**

chicken chili filling

- > **1 tablespoon vegetable oil**
- > **1 onion, finely chopped**
- > **2 cloves garlic, crushed**
- > **500 g/1 lb lean minced chicken**
- > **1 teaspoon Mexican chili powder**
- > **1/2 cup/125 ml/4 fl oz water**
- > **2 tablespoons tomato paste (purée)**
- > **freshly ground black pepper**
- > **2 tablespoons chopped fresh coriander**

tip from the chef

Lean beef or turkey mince make tasty alternatives to the chicken in this recipe. Mexican chili powder is a mixture of ground chilies and other spices such as cumin. If it is unavailable ordinary chili powder can be used but reduce the amount to suit your taste.

chicken
tetrazzini

■■□ | Cooking time: 25 minutes - Preparation time: 20 minutes

ingredients

> **2 cups/250 g/8 oz dried breadcrumbs**
> **1/2 teaspoon freshly ground black pepper**
> **1/2 teaspoon dried ground garlic**
> **1 egg**
> **1 tablespoon Dijon mustard**
> **2 tablespoons vegetable oil**
> **6 boneless chicken breast fillets, skinned and cut into strips**
> **6 large mushrooms, thinly sliced**
> **1 onion, diced**
> **2 tablespoons dry sherry**
> **440 g/14 oz canned condensed cream of mushroom soup**
> **1 cup/250 ml/8 fl oz milk**
> **1 teaspoon Worcestershire sauce**
> **500 g/1 lb pasta of your choice, cooked and kept warm**
> **4 tablespoons grated Parmesan cheese**

method

1. Place breadcrumbs, black pepper and ground garlic in a bowl and toss to combine.
2. Place egg and mustard in a separate bowl and whisk to combine.
3. Heat 1 tablespoon oil in a nonstick frying pan over a medium heat. Dip chicken strips into egg mixture, then toss in breadcrumb mixture to coat. Add chicken to pan and cook, stirring constantly, for 4-5 minutes or until brown. Remove chicken from pan and set aside.
4. Heat remaining oil in pan over a medium heat, add mushrooms and onion and cook, stirring, for 5 minutes. Stir in sherry and cook for 1 minute longer.
5. Stir in soup, milk and Worcestershire sauce and bring to the boil, stirring constantly. Return chicken to pan, reduce heat and simmer for 10 minutes.
6. To serve, divide pasta between serving plates, top with chicken mixture and sprinkle with Parmesan cheese.

....

Serves 6

tip from the chef

Serve with a tossed green salad or steamed vegetables of your choice. Dried ground garlic also called garlic powder is available in the spice section of supermarkets. It has a pungent taste and smell and should be used with care.

spanish
chicken with pine nuts

■ ■ □ | Cooking time: 40 minutes - Preparation time: 15 minutes

method

1. Heat oil in a frying pan over a medium heat, add chicken and cook, turning several times, for 5 minutes or until golden. Add garlic and cook for 5 minutes longer. Transfer chicken and garlic to a flameproof casserole dish.

2. Add onions and green pepper to pan and cook, stirring, for 5 minutes or until onions are golden. Add to casserole dish with chicken.

3. Place casserole over a medium heat and stir in sherry. Bring to the boil, then reduce heat and simmer until liquid is reduced by half. Add stock and black pepper to taste, bring to the boil, then reduce heat, cover and simmer for 25 minutes or until chicken is cooked and tender.

4. To serve, arrange chicken attractively on a serving platter, spoon over sauce and sprinkle with pine nuts and sultanas.

ingredients

> 4 tablespoons olive oil
> 8 chicken thighs, skinned and all visible fat removed
> 2 cloves garlic, crushed
> 4 onions, chopped
> 1 green pepper, diced
> 1/2 cup/125 ml/4 fl oz dry sherry
> 1 cup/250 ml/8 fl oz chicken stock
> freshly ground black pepper
> 60 g/2 oz pine nuts, toasted
> 60 g/2 oz sultanas

....
Serves 4

tip from the chef

Assorted chicken pieces can be used in this dish if you wish.

chili con carne

■ ■ □ | Cooking time: 45 minutes - Preparation time: 15 minutes

method

1. Heat a nonstick saucepan over a medium heat, add beef and cook, stirring, for 4-5 minutes or until meat is brown. Remove beef from pan and set aside.
2. Heat oil in same pan over a medium heat, add onion and cook, stirring, for 4-5 minutes or until onion is golden. Add garlic and chili powder and cook, stirring, for 1 minute.
3. Return meat to pan. Stir in tomatoes, stock and tomato paste (purée) and bring to the boil. Reduce heat, cover and simmer, stirring occasionally, for 30 minutes. Add beans, cumin and black pepper to taste and cook for 5 minutes longer or until heated through.

. . . .

Serves 4

ingredients

> **500 g/1 lb lean beef mince**
> **2 tablespoons vegetable oil**
> **1 onion, diced**
> **3 cloves garlic, crushed**
> **1 tablespoon chili powder or according to taste**
> **2 x 440 g/14 oz canned tomatoes, undrained and mashed**
> **1 cup/250 ml/8 fl oz beef stock**
> **1/4 cup/60 ml/2 fl oz tomato paste (purée)**
> **440 g/14 oz canned red kidney beans, drained and rinsed**
> **1 1/2 teaspoons ground cumin**
> **freshly ground black pepper**

tip from the chef

Keeping some mince in the freezer and cans of beans and tomatoes in the store cupboard gives you the ingredients for a healthy, nutritious meal at a moment's notice. Serve chili con carne on a bed of boiled rice accompanied by a tossed green salad.

lamb
and almond pilau

■■□ I Cooking time: 50 minutes - Preparation time: 20 minutes

ingredients

> **2 tablespoons olive oil**
> **2 tablespoons vegetable oil**
> **3 onions, quartered**
> **500 g/1 lb lean diced lamb**
> **1 cup/220 g/7 oz long-grain rice**
> **3 cups/750 ml/l 1/4 pt boiling chicken or beef stock**
> **1 teaspoon dried thyme**
> **1 teaspoon dried oregano**
> **freshly ground black pepper**
> **125 g/4 oz raisins**
> **60 g/2 oz whole almonds, roasted**

method

1. Heat olive and vegetable oils together in a large saucepan over a low heat, add onions and cook, stirring frequently, for 10 minutes or until onions are golden. Remove from pan and set aside.

2. Increase heat to high and cook lamb in batches for 4-5 minutes or until lamb is well browned. Remove lamb from pan and set aside.

3. Wash rice under cold running water until water runs clears. Drain well. Add rice to pan and cook, stirring constantly, for 5 minutes. Slowly stir boiling stock into pan. Add thyme, oregano and black pepper to taste, then reduce heat, cover pan with a tight-fitting lid and simmer for 20 minutes or until all liquid is absorbed. Return lamb and onions to pan, cover and cook for 5 minutes longer.

4. Remove pan from heat and using a fork fluff up rice mixture. Sprinkle with raisins and almonds and serve.

....
Serves 6

tip from the chef
When cooking pilau it is important that the lid fits tightly on the pan. If the lid does not fit the pan tightly, first cover with aluminum foil, then with the lid.

porcupines

a

■■□ | Cooking time: 30 minutes - Preparation time: 20 minutes

method

1. Place beef, breadcrumbs, ground garlic, paprika, egg and black pepper to taste in a bowl (a) and mix well to combine. Roll mixture into 8 balls then press to form flat patties (b). Roll each pattie in rice to coat (c).
2. Place soup and water in a saucepan, add patties (d), cover and bring to simmering over a low heat. Simmer, stirring occasionally, for 30 minutes or until rice is cooked.

....

Serves 4

ingredients

> **500 g/1 lb lean beef mince**
> **^{1}/4 cup/30 g/1 oz dried breadcrumbs**
> **^{1}/2 teaspoon dried ground garlic**
> **^{1}/2 teaspoon paprika**
> **1 egg, beaten**
> **freshly ground black pepper**
> **^{1}/2 cup/100 g/3^1/2 oz long grain rice**
> **440 g/14 oz canned tomato soup**
> **^{1}/2 cup/125 ml/4 fl oz water**

tip from the chef

It is important when cooking the patties that the soup mixture is barely simmering, if it is boiling the patties will fall apart. For a complete meal serve with steamed vegetables of your choice.

b

c

d

italian pork
with lemon sauce

■■□ I Cooking time: 10 minutes - Preparation time: 20 minutes

ingredients
> flour
> 1 teaspoon dried oregano
> freshly ground black pepper
> 1 egg, beaten
> 1 tablespoon cold water
> dried breadcrumbs
> 8 pork schnitzels or 4 butterfly pork steaks, lightly pounded
> vegetable oil

lemon butter sauce
> 2 teaspoons butter
> 1 tablespoon lemon juice

method
1. Place flour, 1/2 teaspoon oregano and black pepper to taste in a shallow dish and mix to combine. Place egg, water and black pepper to taste in a separate shallow dish and whisk to combine. Place breadcrumbs and remaining oregano in a third shallow dish and mix to combine.
2. Coat pork with flour mixture (a), then dip in egg mixture and finally coat with breadcrumb mixture (b). Place coated pork on a plate lined with plastic food wrap and chill for 10-15 minutes.
3. Heat 2-3 tablespoons oil in a frying pan over a medium-high heat and cook 2-3 schnitzels at a time (c) for 3 minutes each side or cook steaks for 4 minutes each side. Remove pork from pan, set aside and keep warm.
4. To make sauce, melt butter in same pan, then stir in lemon juice (d). Spoon sauce over pork and serve immediately.

....
Serves 4

tip from the chef
When cooking the pork it is important not to crowd the pan or the meat will steam and the coating will be soggy. This is also a delicious way of cooking boneless chicken breast fillets, lightly pounded. The cooking time for chicken will be 4 minutes each side.

a

b

c

d

tandoori
beef burgers

■ ■ □ | Cooking time: 10 minutes - Preparation time: 25 minutes

method

1. To make dressing, place yogurt, coriander, cumin and chili powder to taste in a bowl and mix to combine. Cover and chill until required.
2. To make patties, place beef, garlic, breadcrumbs, egg, Tandoori paste and soy sauce in a bowl and mix to combine. Divide beef mixture into four portions and shape into patties.
3. Heat a little oil in a frying pan over a medium-high heat, add patties and cook for 4-5 minutes each side or until cooked to your liking.
4. Top bottom half of each roll with a lettuce leaf, some tomato slices, 2 cucumber slices, a pattie and a spoonful of dressing. Place other halves on top.

Serves 4

ingredients

> 4 wholemeal bread rolls, split and toasted
> 4 lettuce leaves
> 2 tomatoes, sliced
> 8 slices cucumber

tandoori patties

> 500 g/1 lb lean beef mince
> 2 cloves garlic, crushed
> 2 tablespoons dried breadcrumbs
> 1 egg
> 1 1/2 tablespoons Tandoori paste
> 1 tablespoon soy sauce
> vegetable oil

spiced yogurt dressing

> 1/2 cup/100 g/3 1/2 oz natural yogurt
> 1 tablespoon chopped fresh coriander
> 1/2 teaspoon ground cumin
> pinch chili powder

tip from the chef

These burgers are also delicious made using lamb mince in place of the beef.

american-style
franks and beans

■☐☐ | Cooking time: 20 minutes - Preparation time: 10 minutes

ingredients

> **2 tablespoons vegetable oil**
> **1 onion, diced**
> **4 Continental frankfurters, sliced**
> **2 x 440 g/14 oz canned baked beans**
> **2 tablespoons barbecue sauce**
> **1/2 teaspoon chili powder (optional)**

method

1. Heat oil in a frying pan over a medium heat, add onion and cook, stirring, for 5 minutes or until golden.
2. Add frankfurters and cook, stirring, for 5 minutes longer.
3. Stir in beans, sauce and chili powder, if using, and bring to the boil. Reduce heat and simmer for 10 minutes.

....
Serves 4

tip from the chef

For a complete meal serve on a bed of boiled rice or pasta with steamed green vegetables of your choice. Frankfurters freeze well and are a great standby for those times when you haven't had time to go to the supermarket. Frankfurters can be cooked from frozen, but you will need to increase the cooking by 5-10 minutes.

chinese pork
with spring onions

■■□ | Cooking time: 10 minutes - Preparation time: 25 minutes

method

1. Using a sharp knife, cut pork across the grain into 5 mm/¹⁄₄ in thick slices. Place pork between sheets of greaseproof paper and pound lightly to tenderize and flatten.

2. To make marinade, place cornflour, garlic, soy sauce and sugar in a bowl and mix to combine. Add pork, toss to coat and marinate at room temperature for 20 minutes.

3. Heat oil in a wok or frying pan over a high heat, add pork and stir-fry for 5 minutes or until pork is tender.

4. Add spring onions, chili, soy sauce and sherry and stir-fry for 1-2 minutes. Serve immediately.

ingredients

> **500 g/1 lb pork fillet**
> **3 tablespoons vegetable oil**
> **4 spring onions, thinly sliced**
> **1 red chili, seeded and diced**
> **1 tablespoon soy sauce**
> **1 teaspoon sherry**

marinade

> **1 tablespoon cornflour**
> **2 cloves garlic, crushed**
> **1 tablespoon soy sauce**
> **2 teaspoons sugar**

....

Serves 4

tip from the chef

For a complete meal accompany with steamed vegetables of your choice and boiled rice or Oriental noodles.

mongolian lamb

■ ■ ☐ | Cooking time: 15 minutes - Preparation time: 15 minutes

method

1. To make sauce, place cornflour in a small bowl, then stir in soy sauce, oyster sauce and stock. Set aside.
2. Heat oil in a wok or frying pan over a medium heat, add lamb and stir-fry for 3-4 minutes or until it just changes color. Remove lamb from pan and set aside.
3. Add onions to pan and stir-fry for 2-3 minutes. Add spring onions, garlic and chilies and stir-fry for 2 minutes.
4. Return lamb to pan, add sauce and cook, stirring, for 2-3 minutes or until mixture thickens slightly. Sprinkle with coriander and serve immediately.

....
Serves 4

ingredients

> **2 tablespoons vegetable oil**
> **500 g/1 lb lamb fillet, cut into paper-thin slices**
> **2 onions, cut into 8 wedges**
> **4 spring onions, chopped**
> **3 cloves garlic, crushed**
> **2 small fresh red chilies, seeded and chopped**
> **1 tablespoon chopped fresh coriander**

mongolian sauce

> **2$^1/2$ teaspoons cornflour**
> **1$^1/2$ tablespoons light soy sauce**
> **1 tablespoon oyster sauce**
> **$^1/2$ cup/125 ml/4 fl oz chicken stock**

tip from the chef

When handling fresh chilies do not put your hands near your eyes or allow them to touch your lips. To avoid discomfort and burning, you might like to wear rubber gloves. Bottled minced chilies, available from supermarkets and Oriental food shops, are a convenient product that can be substituted for fresh chilies.

peach
and strawberry pizza

■□□ | Cooking time: 10 minutes - Preparation time: 10 minutes

method

1. Place butter, sugar, flour and cinnamon in a bowl and mix to make a mixture with a crumble consistency.
2. Heat pikelets or drop scones under a preheated medium grill for 1 minute or until just warm.
3. Turn pikelets or drop scones over, spread with conserve, then top with peach halves and sprinkle with butter mixture. Return to grill and cook for 5 minutes or until top is golden.

ingredients

> 30 g/1 oz unsalted butter, softened
> 3 tablespoons brown sugar
> 2 tablespoons flour
> 1/2 teaspoon ground cinnamon
> 8 prepared pikelets or drop scones
> strawberry conserve
> 440 g/14 oz canned peach halves, drained

....
Serves 4

tip from the chef

Sensational served with whipped cream or vanilla ice cream. Any combination of jam or conserve and fruit can be used. You might like to try blackcurrant jam with apples.

new orleans-style bananas

■□□ I Cooking time: 10 minutes - Preparation time: 10 minutes

method

1. Melt butter in a heavy-based frying pan over a medium heat, add sugar and cinnamon and cook, stirring, until sugar melts and mixture is combined.
2. Stir in liqueur or orange juice and half the rum and cook for 5 minutes or until mixture is thick and syrupy.
3. Add bananas and toss to coat with syrup. Add remaining rum, swirl pan and ignite immediately. Baste bananas with sauce until flame goes out.
4. To serve, divide bananas and ice cream between serving plates and drizzle sauce from pan over ice cream. Serve immediately.

ingredients

> **60 g/2 oz unsalted butter**
> **¹/₃ cup/60 g/2 oz brown sugar**
> **¹/₂ teaspoon ground cinnamon**
> **¹/₄ cup/60 ml/2 fl oz banana-flavored liqueur or orange juice**
> **¹/₂ cup/125 ml/4 fl oz dark rum**
> **4 bananas, halved lengthwise**
> **4 scoops vanilla ice cream**

....
Serves 4

tip from the chef

For a non-alcohol dessert, replace liqueur and rum with half orange and half lemon juice. If making the non-alcoholic version, you will not be able to flambé this dessert.

index

Introduction 3

Sandwiches
New York Reuben 8
The BLTA 6
Sun & Moon... 10

Pasta
Curried Pasta Salad 12
Noodles with Coconut Sauce 18
Pasta Putanesca 16
Pesto Pasta... 14

Vegetables
Crusty Corn Soufflé 20
Potato Latkes with Salsa Fresca 26
Ratatouille.. 22
Spicy Vegetable Burgers........................... 24

Cheese and Eggs
French Fried Camembert............................ 30
Ranch-style Eggs 28

Fish
Bengal Fish with Yogurt 36
Cajun Blackened Fish 34
Fillets of Fish Florentine 32

Chicken
Chicken Tacos 38
Chicken Tetrazzini 40
Spanish Chicken with Pine Nuts 42

Meat
American-style Franks and Beans................ 54
Chili con Carne 44
Chinese Pork with Spring Onions 56
Italian Pork with Lemon Sauce 50
Lamb and Almond Pilau............................ 46
Mongolian Lamb 58
Porcupines 48
Tandoori Beef Burgers 52

Desserts
New Orleans-style Bananas 62
Peach and Strawberry Pizza....................... 60